The Great Unicorn Roundup

Charlie Bacon

The Great Unicorn Roundup

by Gary Hogg

ILLUSTRATED BY ELISE SUMMERS

Little Buckaroo Books

Text copyright © 2019 by Gary Hogg
Illustrations copyright © by Elise Summers
Designed by Matt Shay
ISBN 978-0930771447

Printed in the U.S.A.

10 9 8 7 6 5 4 3 2 1

For Sara Good
A girl who loves all
adorable,
snuggly,
creepy,
crawly,
prickly,
monstrous,
minuscule,
strange,
and
magical
creatures.

Contents

Chapter 1
Horrible Hank

"I am never getting married!" announced Charlie Bacon.

"That's not what I heard," said his big sister, Shrudi. "A little birdie told me that you and Allison from your class were getting engaged."

"I am not engaging Allison!" blurted Charlie. "Don't ever say that again."

Shrudi giggled and announced, "I will never say Charlie is marrying Allison…even though it's true."

"Do I have permission to punch Shrudi?" asked Charlie.

Mom turned to look at her three children in the

back seat of the family's car.

"Just once I'd like to make the trip to Uncle Mike's farm without any fighting," said Mom. "We're going to a wedding. We need L-O-V-E."

Lottie was Charlie's mom's little sister and Charlie's favorite aunt. She was marrying Rob the next day. Their wedding was going to be in Uncle Mike's big barn.

"I think getting married in a barn is weird," said Shrudi. "It smells like pig poo."

"When we get done cleaning and decorating it will look and smell beautiful," said Mom.

"There won't be any pigs at my wedding. I'm getting married in a magical castle," insisted Shrudi.

"I bet you marry a pig," joked Charlie.

"I will marry a prince not a pig," argued Shrudi.

"Pig," said Charlie.

"Prince," repeated Shrudi.

"Pig."

"Prince."

"Pig."

"Prince."

"Pig."

"Prince."

"That's enough," said Dad. "We'll love whoever Shrudi marries."

"What if she really marries a pig? One with a curly tail and a snout and pig ears," laughed Charlie.

"Then we'll love him," said Dad.

"I AM NOT MARRYING A PIG!" yelled Shrudi.

As Charlie's dad steered the car into the long lane leading to Uncle Mike's farm, Charlie sat up to see if he could spot his cousin Hank. Hank was famous for his weird and wild ways of welcoming the Bacon family to the farm.

Once for a Halloween visit, Hank used a gigantic slingshot to launch a storm of underwear that rained down on the Bacon family car. Another time he dressed as Tarzan and swung from a rope to the top of the car. The car still had two dents on the roof from where he landed.

Charlie's favorite escapade was when Hank hooked a siren and flashing light to his souped-up riding lawnmower, The Chopper. As Charlie's dad drove down the lane Hank roared out from behind a tree and arrested the entire Bacon family. Dad had to pay a speeding fine of five dollars, which Hank used to buy milkshakes for Charlie and himself.

Dad cautiously pulled up and parked in front of Uncle Mike's house.

"This is strange," said Mom. "No sign of Hank."

"Maybe they put Horrible Hank in prison where he

belongs," said Shrudi.

"I think we're safe," said Dad as he got out of the car. Mom got out next and slowly turned in a circle, searching the shrubs and trees for any kind of surprise attack.

"You might be right," she said.

Shrudi and Charlie had just gotten out of the car when the barn door flew open. Hank came stampeding out on a white pony. His black cowboy hat was pulled down tight and he was swinging a rope.

"Stay away from me!" shouted Shrudi, scrambling onto the hood of the car.

"Rope her!" cheered Charlie as Hank charged across the lawn.

Hank's horse jumped the flower bed and galloped straight for the Bacon's car. After three laps around the car Hank skidded his horse to a stop. The pony

pranced in place and Hank tipped his hat.

"You could have killed someone," snapped Shrudi.

"It's nice to see you too," replied Hank.

Charlie's little brother, Jimmy, squirmed out of his car seat and plopped to the ground. He held up his arms and wiggled his fingers.

Mom laughed and said, "Someone wants a ride."

Charlie's dad picked Jimmy up so he could pet the pony's soft nose.

"What's his name?" asked Charlie.

"Her name is Tilly. She's my new roping horse," said Hank. "Climb on behind me and I'll give you a ride to the house."

Charlie stepped in the stirrup and swung up behind his cousin. Before Charlie could get a grip on the saddle, Hank kicked Tilly and she trotted toward the house.

Charlie bounced to the back of Tilly's rump, startling her. In a flash she kicked up her back legs and started bucking.

"Whoa, girl," said Hank as he tried to gain control.

"Yee-haw!" yelled Charlie. He leaned forward and wrapped his arms around Hank.

Tilly gave one last high kick and both boys slid off onto the ground.

"That was wild!" shouted Charlie. "Let's do it again."

Hank's parents and his sister, Hannah, came out on the front porch when they heard the commotion.

"Hank, your horse is getting away," called Uncle Mike as Tilly trotted around the side of the house.

Hank jumped up and ran after his pony. Charlie dusted himself off and began to follow Hank when Mom stopped him.

"Not so fast, Buckaroo, you need to help unload the car," she said.

Charlie's dad grabbed two suitcases while Mom took hold of Jimmy's hand. The three of them headed to the house.

Hannah ran up to Shrudi and gave her a hug.

"We're going to be flower girls," sang Shrudi.

"Do you have your dress?" asked Hannah.

"It's so pretty," answered Shrudi, pulling a garment bag out of the trunk.

"Let's go put them on," said Hannah.

The girls hurried away, giggling with excitement.

Charlie was all alone when he heard a noise. He looked up to see a bright yellow unicorn zooming toward the house.

Chapter 2
The Ring Bear

The shiny yellow Volkswagen Beetle had a custom license plate that read UNICORN. A hot pink unicorn horn was attached to the front of the hood. The driver wore sunglasses and her hair was colored lavender.

The stereo was blasting when the unicorn car slid to a stop in front of the house. Charlie's eyes widened when he recognized Aunt Lottie. She jumped out and gave Charlie a tight hug.

"How do you like my new ride?" she asked.

"It's pretty unicorny," said Charlie.

"I know," said Lottie laughing. "Unicorns are my lucky charms."

"Mine too," fibbed Charlie.

Hank came galloping around the house on Tilly.

"Hey, cowboy!" called out Lottie.

Hank reined Tilly to the Beetle and stopped. He dismounted and gave his aunt a high five.

"Is this your new horse?" she asked.

"This is Tilly," said Hank. "Do you want to go for a ride?"

Aunt Lottie didn't answer. She just swung into the saddle and galloped off.

"Someday I'm going to marry someone just like her," said Hank. He took his rope and spun out a loop. After three twirls of the rope he lassoed the unicorn horn on Aunt Lottie's car.

"Sweet action," said Charlie. "Can you teach me to rope like that?"

"I'm planning on it," said Hank as he roped the

horn a second time.

Tilly trotted up to the boys.

"She's a nice little mare," Lottie said, sliding out of the saddle. "If she had a unicorn horn on her head she'd be perfect."

"Tilly is better than any unicorn," said Hank. "Unicorns are make-believe."

"Are you telling me you've never heard of Butterfly Valley?" asked Lottie.

She pointed to a nearby mountain and said, "On the other side of Middle Fork Ridge is Butterfly Valley. Each year thousands of monarch butterflies fill the valley during their yearly migration."

"What does that have to do with unicorns?" asked Charlie.

"Unicorns and butterflies are best friends. When the butterflies arrive, the unicorns join them," said

Lottie. "When I was a little girl I used to dream of catching a unicorn."

"If I ever see one, I'll rope it for you," bragged Hank.

"That would be the best wedding present ever," said Lottie.

"I'll rope one for you too," added Charlie.

"Wow, two unicorns," said Aunt Lottie laughing. "I can't wait."

While Hank led Tilly to the corral, Aunt Lottie said to Charlie, "You know we are both named after the same person, Grandma Charlotte. Some people called her Charlie and some called her Lottie.

"Sharing the name of such a wonderful person is a very special thing to me so I'd like you to do something important at my wedding. During the wedding I want you to come down the aisle carrying a pillow that holds the rings. I want you to be the ring bearer."

"The ring bear," said Charlie. "Do I get to growl and wear a suit?"

"You wear a suit but you don't need to growl," said Aunt Lottie.

"I could grunt if you don't like growling," said Charlie.

"Definitely no grunting," said Aunt Lottie. "But you'll need a suit."

"No problem," said Charlie. "I'll get the best suit you've ever seen."

Charlie quickly unloaded the trunk and carried the bags into the house. He then raced outside to find Hank.

"Guess what? I get to dress up as a bear for the wedding," said Charlie. "Do you have a bear suit I can borrow?"

"I'm fresh out of bear suits but I have something even better. I have a Sasquatch costume," said Hank.

"Aunt Lottie wants me to be the ring bear. I don't know if she would want me to be a Sasquatch," said Charlie.

Hank took Charlie into his bedroom and opened the closet.

"Wow, your closet is messier than mine. I didn't think that was possible," said Charlie.

"It's all organized," explained Hank. "I have a system. The right side is for stuff that smells bad and the left side is for things that smell really bad."

"Where's the Sasquatch suit?" asked Charlie.

"Oh, it smells very bad," said Hank. "So it's on the left side."

Like a mole digging a new tunnel, Hank burrowed

in headfirst through the assortment of toys, clothes, and garbage. Soon all that was sticking out were his legs.

"Pull," came a muffled scream from inside the smelly pile.

Charlie got a grip on Hank's legs and began to pull. With a sturdy tug, Charlie jerked Hank out of the mess. Hank was holding a suit of dirty brown hair.

"Meet Sasquatch," said Hank proudly.

Charlie took a whiff and wrinkled his nose.

"It certainly smells like Sasquatch," said Charlie.

"Just like the real deal. There's a mask and gloves too," said Hank proudly.

Charlie pulled the heavy costume on over the top of his clothes and slid his hands into the gloves. When he tried to put on the mask, it wouldn't slide over his head. He pulled harder but still no luck.

"It's too small," complained Charlie.

"No it's not," said Hank. "We just need some butter."

Charlie followed Hank into the kitchen.

"Everything's better with butter," said Hank as he began rubbing soft, creamy butter into Charlie's hair and down his forehead.

"You're good to go," said Hank, licking the extra butter off his fingers.

Charlie pulled on the mask and it slipped over his greasy hair and onto his head.

"You look fantastic," said Hank, grinning.

"Do you think Aunt Lottie will like it?" asked Charlie.

"Like it? She's going to LOVE it," said Hank.

Chapter 3
I Look Weird

Sasquatch Charlie and Hank paraded down the hall and into the living room.

Hank sang, "Here comes the Sasquatch. All dressed in hair. He carries the ring. Because he's the ring bear."

Aunt Sheila, Charlie's mom, and Aunt Lottie were sitting on the couch discussing decorations for the wedding when the boys marched in. All three ladies started laughing.

"What on earth are you two up to?" asked Aunt Sheila between giggles.

"I couldn't find a bear suit but I hope this is close enough," said Charlie.

Charlie's mom looked confused and asked, "Why do you need a bear suit?"

"Because I'm the ring bear," said Charlie.

"You're the ring bearer, not ring bear," explained Mom.

Lottie laughed louder and said, "When I said suit, I meant a tuxedo. Your mom already has it."

"I have to get a picture of this," said Aunt Sheila, grabbing her phone. "I can't wait to post it."

After Aunt Sheila snapped some pictures, Charlie's mom opened a garment bag and took out a midnight black tuxedo.

"This is the suit you'll wear for the wedding," she said.

Charlie pulled the Sasquatch mask off to get a better look at the tuxedo.

"What's in your hair?" asked his mother. "It smells

like butter."

"The mask was too tight so I buttered him up a bit," said Hank. "I only used a handful."

"It's pretty fancy," said Charlie, examining the tuxedo. "Are you sure it will fit me?"

"Let's find out," said Mom. "Get cleaned up and we'll have a little fashion show."

Charlie hurried into the bathroom to take a shower. After a good scrubbing, he dried himself off and poked his head out the door.

"I'm ready for the tuxedo," Charlie called to his mother.

Charlie's mom came into the bathroom to help him get dressed. She buttoned the white shirt and attached a bright red bow tie to the collar. The shiny black pants, coat, and vest fit perfectly. After putting on a pair of new black shoes, Charlie felt like a movie star.

His mother combed his hair and followed him out of the bathroom. Charlie walked into the living room to model his new look. He was surprised to find the room full of people. Everyone but Hank had gathered to get a sneak peek of the ring bearer.

Charlie strutted to the center of the room and did a quick turn before stopping to pose.

"Who are you and what did you do with my brother?" asked Shrudi.

"You look handsome," said Hannah.

Charlie blushed and walked across the room a second time before doing another turn and flashing his biggest smile.

"I think he likes this new look," said Aunt Lottie.

"No I don't," fibbed Charlie. "I look weird."

Aunt Lottie gave Charlie a hug and said, "You look perfect."

"Go change back into your regular clothes," said Charlie's mom. "We want the tuxedo to look brand new for the wedding."

Charlie looked out the window and saw Hank spinning his rope.

"Can I show it to Hank?" asked Charlie.

"OK, but then come right back and put on your play clothes," said Mom.

Charlie's mom and two aunts went back to planning the wedding decorations while Charlie hurried out the front door. He ran over to where Hank was roping a bucket.

"Good loop," said Charlie as Hank roped the bucket.

Hank looked at Charlie's tuxedo and said, "Nice penguin suit, but I prefer something a little more cowboy looking."

Hank made another loop and zipped the rope on the bucket again.

"Can I try?" asked Charlie.

"Sure," said Hank, handing the rope to Charlie.

Charlie tried to spin the loop but got all tangled up.

"It's harder than it looks," he said.

Hank showed Charlie how to hold the rope and twirl the loop to keep it from getting tangled up. Soon Charlie was roping the bucket.

"Hey, you're pretty good," said Hank. "But if we're going to rope unicorns we're going to have to practice roping something that can run faster than a bucket."

"What do you have in mind?" asked Charlie.

"Our pigs, Ethel and Lucy, are pretty lazy except at feeding time," said Hank. "Chickens are fast but their heads are too small. We need something with horns."

Hank rubbed his chin as he thought. When he looked into the pasture he announced, "I've got it! We can rope Wart."

"Oh no, not Wart," said Charlie, shaking his head. "He's a killer."

Wart was a mean old ram that had long curled horns. He would chase anyone who bothered him. And everyone bothered him.

The boys walked over to the pasture behind the barn. Wart was relaxing in his favorite spot under a huge willow tree.

"That old sheep is as cranky as they come," said Hank. "We'll need to be pretty light on our feet to keep from getting one of his horns in our backsides."

"It looks like he's sleeping," said Charlie. "We can sneak up on him."

Hank opened the gate and entered the pasture.

When Charlie hesitated, Hank said, "Come on, we don't have all day."

"I better go change my clothes. Mom will kill me if I get my tuxedo dirty," said Charlie.

"We don't have time," said Hank. "Wart will wake up any minute. I promise you won't get dirty. It's just a little roping."

Charlie followed Hank into the pasture and closed the gate.

Chapter 4

Roping a Monster

"You're going to be the bait," said Hank.

"I don't like the sound of that," said Charlie. "Doesn't the bait usually get eaten?"

"Relax, Twinkle Toes," said Hank. "I'll rope him before he even gets close to you."

Hank stopped thirty feet from where Wart was sleeping.

"I'll stay here and you go get Wart to chase you. Run past me and I'll snag the old boy with a quick loop," said Hank.

"What should I do if you miss?" asked Charlie.

"Run in a circle and I'll rope him on the next

round," said Hank. "But I hardly ever miss."

Charlie stopped ten feet from the sleeping ram and said, "Wakey-Wakey."

The huge sheep kept sleeping. Charlie turned around to Hank and joked, "I think he's counting sheep."

"Not anymore!" shouted Hank. "Look behind you!"

Charlie glanced over his shoulder to see the ram charging him like a locomotive.

"Oh no!" yelled Charlie as he sprinted away, barely avoiding Wart's horns.

"Bring him to daddy!" hollered Hank as he twirled the rope over his head.

Charlie zoomed past his cousin with the ram hot on his heels. Hank tossed a quick loop but barely grazed the sheep's curled horns.

Charlie turned a tight circle and Hank took a

second throw. This time the loop flew right around Wart's horns.

"I got him!" yelled Hank as he braced his feet in the grass.

When the ram came to the end of the rope, he didn't even slow down. Hank did a Superman take-off and flew six feet in the air before belly flopping onto the grass. Charlie looked over his shoulder to see Hank being dragged behind the powerful ram.

"Hang on!" shouted Charlie.

Charlie turned and headed straight for an irrigation ditch that ran across the bottom of the pasture.

"The water in the ditch will slow him down," yelled Charlie.

Hank's face was being weed whacked as the sheep pulled him across the field. He bounced and crashed across the pasture like a rag doll.

Charlie took a giant leap but missed clearing the ditch by a foot. He landed in the dirty water with a splash. Wart slid to a stop on the bank of the ditch and snorted as he eyeballed Charlie.

When the old sheep dropped his horns and headed into the ditch, Charlie tried to get up but his feet were stuck in the black mud. Wart suddenly stopped and dropped his head into the ditch to suck in a long drink of cool water.

Charlie eased the rope off Wart's horns before the ram turned and moseyed back to his favorite spot under the tree.

Hank slowly got to his feet and staggered over to the ditch. He plopped into the dirty water next to Charlie.

"I guess we showed him who's boss around here," said Hank, pulling a dandelion out of his nose.

"We sure did," answered Charlie.

The boys helped each other out of the muddy water. Standing next to the ditch, Charlie examined his mud-covered tuxedo.

"This is your fault," said Charlie. "I should never have listened to you."

"My fault?" gasped Hank. "You're the one who jumped in the ditch."

"I was trying to save your life!" argued Charlie.

"OK, relax," said Hank. "I'll fix it."

"How are you going to fix it?" asked Charlie.

"Don't worry," said Hank. "We'll hose it off and hang it out to dry."

"If we hang it up to dry, someone will see it for sure," complained Charlie.

"Settle down," said Hank. "The tuxedo will be hiding in plain sight."

"I don't even know what that means," said Charlie.

"It means I have a plan," said Hank.

Hank led Charlie to the garden and used the hose to wash away the mud. Standing guard in the garden was a scarecrow that was dressed like a pirate.

"We'll just let Blackbeard wear the tuxedo while it dries," said Hank. "Nobody but the birds ever pay attention to him."

Hank removed Blackbeard's tattered clothes and handed them to Charlie.

After a quick change of clothes Charlie gave the tuxedo to Hank. Soon Blackbeard was the world's best dressed scarecrow.

"What do we do now?" asked Charlie.

Hank sat down in the grass and said, "Now we wait and let the sun do its magic."

They didn't wait very long. The back door opened

and out came Charlie's mom and Aunt Lottie. Mom spotted the boys and headed straight to the garden.

"There you are," she said. "We've been looking all over the house for you."

Chapter 5

It's a Pirate's Life for Me

Aunt Lottie raised her eyebrows when she spotted Blackbeard. She glanced at Charlie and back at Blackbeard.

Mom squinted her eyes as she looked at Charlie's new outfit.

"Why are you wearing those filthy old clothes?" she asked.

"We're playing pirates," said Charlie, with a half-hearted smile on his face.

"Argh, it's a pirate's life for me," said Hank in his best pirate accent.

Mom rubbed her forehead and wondered out loud,

"Where have I seen those clothes before?"

"You've probably seen me wearing them," fibbed Hank. "They're my old school clothes."

"No, that's not it," said Mom.

Before Mom could turn and look at Blackbeard, Aunt Lottie picked up a stick and shouted, "You blimey scallywags! You'll walk the plank for this!"

She chased Charlie and Hank away from the garden. Mom began laughing as she watched Lottie chase the boys.

"OK, scallywags, I need you two to clean out the barn so we can start decorating," said Mom.

"Now?" moaned Charlie. "I was about to become the pirate king."

"Right now," said Mom. "Dad and Uncle Mike have already removed all the equipment. There are some straw bales next to the wall. Leave them there and clean everything else out."

Aunt Lottie waited until Mom was in the house and said, "Those are some pretty fancy clothes for a scarecrow."

"It's my ring bearer suit," confessed Charlie.

"I can see that," said Lottie. "Why is the scarecrow wearing your tuxedo? And why is it soaking wet?"

"We were roping Wart and I accidently fell in the ditch," said Charlie. "We put the clothes on Blackbeard so they could dry in the sun."

Aunt Lottie rubbed her eyes and said, "OK, boys, here's the deal. This wedding is really stressing me out."

"Then don't marry Rob," said Hank. "Someone better will come along."

"Oh, I love Rob. He doesn't stress me out," said Lottie. "But surprises such as finding the ring bearer's tuxedo on a scarecrow stress me. Do you understand?"

"I get it," said Charlie. "Blackbeard is not invited to the wedding."

"No," said Lottie. "Less mess equals less stress."

"We got it," said Hank. "We'll start by cleaning out the barn."

"Perfect," said Lottie. "I'll take care of the tuxedo. Put it in the back seat of my car."

Charlie went into the bathroom to change back into his clothes while Hank took the tuxedo off of Blackbeard and placed it in Aunt Lottie's car. By the time Charlie had dressed Blackbeard in the pirate clothes, Hank was waiting for him in the barn.

Charlie looked around the huge building and complained, "This is going to take forever."

To pass time while they cleaned, Charlie and Hank made up a rhyming game.

"Can you rope a duck?" asked Charlie.

"With a little luck," answered Hank.

"Can you rope a horse?" asked Charlie.

"Of course," bragged Hank.

"Can you rope a fly?" asked Charlie.

"Right out of the sky," laughed Hank.

"Can you rope a cat?" asked Charlie.

"Just like that," answered Hank.

"Can you rope a mouse?" asked Charlie.

"Only in the house," said Hank.

Finally, the barn's floor was swept and four big garbage bags were filled with trash. Charlie plopped down on one of the straw bales to rest. When he looked behind the bale, his eyes grew to the size of saucers.

"Can you rope a skunk?" asked Charlie.

Before Hank could answer, Charlie said, "I just saw a skunk go into a hole between these straw bales."

Hank sucked in a deep breath and asked, "Are you sure it was a skunk? Maybe it was a cat."

"Do you have a black cat that has two white stripes down its back?" asked Charlie.

"Our cat, Doofus, is yellow," said Hank.

"Then it's a skunk for sure," said Charlie.

"Come on," said Hank as he raced for the door. "I have been waiting for this moment my whole life."

Charlie hustled to keep up.

"Where are we going?" he asked.

"To my secret lab," answered Hank.

Chapter 6
Mr. Stinky Pants

The boys raced through the back door of the house and sprinted down the stairs to the basement.

Hank let out an evil scientist laugh when they reached the door of Dr. Hankenstein's Secret Lab. He shoved the door open and pulled the string that turned on the light.

Hank grabbed a tall bucket. He put it on his workbench and pulled off the lid.

"I have plans for a skunk trap in here somewhere," he said. "Trapping and training a troop of skunks is on my bucket list."

"What's a bucket list?" asked Charlie.

Hank let out a huff of air and explained, "This is a bucket. Inside are lists of things I want to do."

Charlie unfolded the first piece of paper and read, "Invent a gas-powered car. I think someone has already beat you to this one. Most cars already run on gas."

"My car won't run on gasoline. It'll be powered by human gas. The driver and passengers supply the gas, which will be collected through funnels in the seats.

The gas goes into a master flatulator that sends the gas to the engine. I'm calling it the Tootermobile."

"This is brilliant," said Charlie. "The sale of chili beans is going to go through the roof."

"I only have one problem left to solve," said Hank.

"What's that?" asked Charlie.

"Air pollution," said Hank. "The fumes are going to be horrible."

Charlie thought for a moment and then suggested, "What if you collected the exhaust in balloons and sold them as stink bombs?"

Hank nodded his head and said, "I love the way you think. Together we're going to be zillionaires."

The boys rifled through the papers. Reaching to the bottom of the bucket Hank pulled out a bright pink sheet of paper.

"Here it is!" he announced.

Hank unfolded the paper and placed it on the workbench. Charlie scratched his head as he read the directions for building the trap.

"This is going to take forever," said Charlie. "I have a better idea."

Charlie looked around the lab and found what he was looking for. In the corner was a black storage container with a lid. He pulled off the lid and poured the contents onto the floor.

Charlie grabbed a screwdriver and hammer from a toolbox and punched a series of small holes in the side of the plastic container.

"There's your skunk trap," said Charlie. "It's an old-fashioned box trap. Grandpa showed me how to make one so I could catch a chipmunk when we were camping.

"First, place the box upside down on top of the lid.

Then use a stick to prop up one side of the box for a trigger. Finally, tie a string with a little bit of bait to the stick. The skunk goes into the box to eat the bait, which pulls the trigger. The box falls over the skunk and it's trapped. We push the container down on the lid until it locks in place. The holes in the side of the container let in air so the skunk can breathe."

Hank picked up a large brown bottle and said, "We'll need this anti-stinkum elixir for when the skunk sprays."

"Grandpa told me that a skunk won't spray what it can't see. It'll be dark in the trap so we can carry the skunk around without getting gassed," said Charlie.

Hank gave Charlie a high five and said, "You take the trap to the barn and I'll go get some bait and meet you there."

Charlie had the trap propped up and ready next to

the stack of straw bales when Hank showed up with the bait.

"That is smelly," said Charlie. "What is it?"

"This, my friend, is a sardine. My dad has cans of these little fish in his hiking backpack. He eats them with crackers when he goes camping with his buddies," said Hank.

"Is there only one in a can?" asked Charlie.

"No, there are a bunch. I dumped the rest of them in the backpack. Dad will find them when he goes camping in a couple of weeks," said Hank. "He'll be glad I opened the can for him."

"Good thinking," said Charlie.

After the trap was set, Hank and Charlie tiptoed to the other side of the barn and sat down.

"Keep an eye on the trap," said Hank. "We don't want to miss the action."

The boys stared patiently at the trap. Charlie was the first one to nod off. Hank leaned his head on Charlie's shoulder and soon he was asleep as well.

The sound of the trap snapping shut woke them up.

"We got one!" shouted Charlie.

The boys hurried over and examined the skunk trap. Charlie pushed down on the container until he heard the lid snap shut. As he turned the trap over, Charlie could feel the skunk squirming around.

"Can you see him?" asked Hank.

"No, but I can tell he's a big one," said Charlie.

"This is perfect," said Hank. "I'm going to name him Mr. Stinky Pants and train him to do tricks. We're going to be famous!"

"Let's go tell everybody," said Charlie excitedly.

"Not so fast," said Hank. "We can't tell anyone. There's no way my mom will let me keep a skunk. But after I've trained him she'll have to say yes. I might even teach him how to do a few chores around the house."

The boys turned when they heard footsteps. A tall, dark-haired man was coming through the barn doors.

"Hi, Rob," said Hank.

"I thought Lottie might be in here getting things ready for the wedding," said Rob.

"She's in the house," said Charlie. "She'll be excited to see you."

Right on cue, Aunt Lottie came running into the barn. She hugged Rob and gave him a kiss.

"I saw your truck parked in the front and tracked you down. What do you think of the barn?" asked Lottie.

Rob looked around the huge room and exclaimed, "I love it!"

Lottie pointed to the stack of straw bales and said, "We're going to place these in rows and cover them with quilts. That's where the guests will sit."

"Boys, do you want to help me move the bales?" asked Rob.

"You can move them after lunch," said Aunt Lottie. "Jeff has barbequed some burgers and made his famous coleslaw to go with them."

Aunt Lottie hooked her arm in Rob's arm and escorted him out of the barn. Hank picked up the storage container and began to follow.

"We'll hide Mr. Stinky Pants in the house until after lunch," said Hank.

"Good idea," said Charlie. "We can start training him right after we eat."

Chapter 7
The Eyebrow Extravaganza

While Rob and Lottie went into the kitchen, Hank and Charlie sneaked down the hall and hid Mr. Stinky Pants in the hall closet.

"No one ever looks in here," said Hank. "Mom uses it to store her old junk."

By the time the boys made their way to the kitchen, Charlie's dad was serving burgers and coleslaw.

"Get them while they're hot," said Dad. "There's a veggie burger for you, Lottie."

"What's for dessert?" asked Charlie in between bites of his burger.

"Lottie's making homemade huckleberry ice

cream," announced Dad.

"It's Grandma Charlotte's recipe," said Aunt Lottie. "I thought we could enjoy her favorite ice cream as a way to remember her."

"Can I help?" asked Shrudi.

"Me too?" added Hannah.

"Sure," said Lottie.

Shrudi, Hannah, and Aunt Lottie mixed the ingredients for the ice cream and poured them in a large silver canister. Lottie placed the lid on the canister and set it in a large bucket.

"Now we have to pack layers of ice and salt around the canister until the bucket is full," said Lottie.

After Shrudi and Hannah had filled the bucket with ice and salt, Aunt Lottie attached a motor to the top of the canister and turned it on. The canister started spinning.

Like a bulldog waiting for a doggie treat, Charlie could feel the drool building in his mouth.

"Is it done yet?" he asked.

"Nope," said Aunt Lottie.

"How about now?" asked Hank.

"Be patient," said Lottie.

"Is it done now?" asked Charlie.

Aunt Lottie sighed and said, "No."

"How about now?" asked Hank.

"When the canister stops spinning, the ice cream will be done," said Lottie.

"Is it done now?" asked Charlie.

Aunt Lottie folded her arms and didn't respond.

"How about now?" asked Hank.

"What about now?" asked Charlie.

"You two loony birds are driving everyone nuts," said Charlie's dad.

Charlie looked down at the metal container rotating in the mixture of salt and ice. It began turning slower and slower until it abruptly stopped.

"Now it's done," announced Aunt Lottie.

Soon the family had gathered in the living room to enjoy the huckleberry ice cream.

"Living the dream eating ice cream," said Charlie's mom. "Grandma Charlotte used to say that every time she made ice cream."

"She was a true unicorn," said Aunt Lottie. "She lived life without worrying about what other people thought about her."

"I remember she'd always wear wild-colored silk scarves on her head," Uncle Mike said.

"Didn't she like her hair?" asked Hannah.

Uncle Mike laughed and said, "She didn't have any hair. She was as bald as a bowling ball and it didn't matter. We loved her just the way she was."

"She didn't have any eyebrows either," said Charlie's mom. "Every morning she would take a makeup pencil and draw her eyebrows. But she never drew them the same two days in a row.

"Some days they would arch high up on her forehead so she looked like she was surprised about everything. Other days they would be short and turned down like two worried worms resting on her forehead.

"One day she drew one long unibrow all the way across her forehead with fancy curls on each end."

Shrudi and Hannah were laughing so hard melted ice cream was running down their chins.

"When I was a kindergartener I wanted to be just like her," said Aunt Lottie. "On my birthday I sneaked a blue marker into my backpack and took it to school.

Before school began I drew two humongous eyebrows on my forehead."

"What did your teacher say?" asked Charlie.

"She was surprised to say the least," said Lottie. "At recess Marty Briggs borrowed my marker and drew big eyebrows on his forehead too. One by one the other kindergarteners took turns with the marker. It was an eyebrow extravaganza.

"There were squiggly brows, flowery brows, bold brows, jack-o-lantern brows and twirly curly brows. One boy's monster-sized eyebrows nearly covered his whole forehead.

"When we came back to class after recess, our teacher almost came unglued. She was so upset that she forgot about my birthday celebration until Grandma Charlotte came waltzing into the classroom. She was carrying a tub of her famous huckleberry ice cream and enough bowls and spoons for everyone."

"What'd your teacher do?" asked Charlie.

"What else could she do?" said Lottie. "She drew two eyebrows on her forehead and enjoyed the ice cream."

Rob got up and asked, "Charlie and Hank, are you ready to move those straw bales?"

"I'll meet you there," said Charlie. "I need one more bowl of ice cream."

"Me too," said Hank.

Rob went out the front door and the boys headed to the kitchen.

While Charlie and Hank were in the kitchen getting more ice cream Aunt Sheila said, "I still have some of Charlotte's scarves in a storage bin in the hall closet. I'm going to wear one to the wedding."

"I want to see them," said Hannah, jumping up and

running down the hall. She came back carrying the black storage bin.

"That's the wrong box," said Aunt Sheila. "They're in a blue box."

Hannah put the storage container down in the middle of the room and motioned for everyone to be quiet.

"There's something moving inside this box," she whispered.

"Open it up and see what it is," said Uncle Mike.

Hank and Charlie walked into the living room just as Hannah was loosening the lid.

"Stop!" yelled Charlie. "There's a skunk in that box!"

Chapter 8
The Fast Talker

Hannah tossed the lid in the air and raced into the kitchen. The whole family followed her.

Aunt Sheila blubbered, "There's a skunk in my house! There's a skunk in my house! There's a skunk in my house!"

Charlie's mom glared at Charlie and blurted, "You don't bring skunks into other people's houses. What were you thinking?"

She didn't really want to know what Charlie was thinking because when he opened his mouth to speak she repeated, "You don't bring skunks into other people's houses."

"Shhh," hushed Uncle Mike. "We need to get it out of the house before it sprays."

When everyone turned to listen to Mike, Charlie's little brother, Jimmy, left the kitchen and walked back into the living room.

"Where's Jimmy?" asked Mom, looking around the room.

When she heard Jimmy say, "Hi, kitty kitty," she gasped.

"Jimmy, come back here right now," ordered Mom. "That's a bad kitty."

Jimmy ignored his mother and climbed into the storage container.

Aunt Lottie didn't hesitate. She charged into the living room and raced to the storage container. She snatched Jimmy out of the box and then froze.

Jimmy was holding a yellow cat.

"Doofus?" said Hannah. "What's Doofus doing with a skunk?"

"There is no skunk," said Aunt Lottie. "Just a cat."

Everyone turned and looked at Charlie.

"Is this your idea of a joke? Because it was not funny. You almost gave us all heart attacks," said Shrudi.

Charlie stammered, and then started talking really fast.

"I can explain. I saw a skunk in the barn. Hank wanted to trap it and train it to do tricks. So we went to his lab where he has a bucket list of things he wants to build like a gas-powered car called the Tootermobile. He also has plans for a skunk trap but it would take too long to build. So I made a box trap out of that storage container. We used a sardine for bait. Don't worry, Uncle Mike, we only used one. Hank left the rest of the sardines in your backpack. While we were waiting for the skunk to get into the trap we fell asleep. The trap woke us up when it slammed closed and I thought we caught a skunk. We didn't look in the trap because we didn't want to get blasted with stink. Hank named the skunk Mr. Stinky Pants and we decided to hide him in the closet until Hank could train him to do tricks. You know the rest. Hannah brought the storage bin into the living room and everyone went bonkers when I yelled that it was a skunk."

"Wait, wait, go back," said Aunt Lottie

"Hank's building a car called the Tootermoblie," said Charlie.

"Not that part, you saw a skunk in the barn?" asked Aunt Lottie.

"Yes," said Charlie. "It went into a hole between the

straw bales."

"Oh no," said Lottie. "Rob's in the barn moving those bales. If that skunk is still there, he's going to get sprayed."

The race was on. Everyone sprinted out the back door and ran toward the barn. Lottie was the first to dash through the barn door. The entire family followed her in.

Rob was lifting a straw bale when they charged into the barn. He set the bale down and turned to the crowd.

"What's up?" he asked.

"That," said Lottie, pointing to a large skunk that had been behind the bale Rob had just lifted. Its tail was straight in the air and its behind was aimed right at Rob.

"Run!" shouted Uncle Mike as the family turned

and dashed back out the door.

The blast that came billowing out of the skunk was massive. The cloud of stink enveloped Rob.

Rob staggered outside and began stumbling around the yard. Aunt Lottie grabbed the hose. She turned the water on and began spraying water directly into Rob's face.

Charlie sprinted into the house and went straight to Hank's bedroom. He quickly pulled on the Sasquatch suit.

In the kitchen, he rubbed his hair with butter and plugged his nostrils with two pieces of tissue. He pulled the mask over his head and slid each hand into a glove.

Feeling like a brand new superhero, Sasquatch Charlie stepped through the back door and marched straight for the barn.

Chapter 9

The Shortcut

When Charlie entered the barn, Mr. Stinky Pants raised his tail and fired another blast of skunk spray. Protected by the Sasquatch costume, Charlie was unstoppable. He marched bravely through the stench.

Before Mr. Stinky Pants could escape, Charlie reached down and picked him up. The skunk squirmed and twisted but Charlie held him tight and carried the smelly troublemaker out of the barn.

"I caught him," yelled Charlie, holding the skunk up high for everyone to see.

"Where do you want him?" he asked as he walked toward Uncle Mike.

Charlie's uncle waved his arms frantically and yelled, "Go the other way! Go the other way!"

"Give him to Wart," shouted Hank as he scrambled to open the gate to the pasture.

Charlie took Mr. Stinky Pants to the willow tree where Wart was sleeping. The mean ram woke up when Charlie placed the skunk down on the ground.

"Meanie meet Stinky. You should get along great," said Charlie.

Wart snorted at the skunk and trotted to the far side of the field while Charlie turned and walked out of the pasture.

"You should take skunk training off your bucket list," said Charlie as he walked past Hank.

"I already have," said Hank. "I'm going to train weasels instead."

Charlie took off the Sasquatch costume and left

it behind the barn. He pulled the tissue out of his nostrils and sucked in a deep breath. The putrid smell of skunk was still floating in the air.

Rob and Lottie were in the backyard. Rob was sitting in the grass. He was coughing and his face was pale. Aunt Lottie was still spraying him with the hose.

Hank came over to Rob and said, "That water is not going to help. You need anti-stinkum elixir. It's the strongest formula known to man. I have a jug of it in my lab."

"I'll try anything," groaned Rob.

Hank retrieved the brown jug and handed it to Rob.

"Don't forget to wash behind your ears," said Hank.

Uncle Mike came out of the house carrying a huge fan. He held it up for Aunt Lottie to see.

"I'm going to try and air the barn out," he said. "Sheila has gone to town to buy every air freshener she can find. Let's keep our fingers crossed that it'll work."

"Fingers, toes, and eyes," said Aunt Lottie as her eyes went crossed.

Charlie and Hank were just turning to leave when Aunt Lottie stopped them.

"Do you boys remember when I said I didn't want any more surprises?" she asked.

Both boys nodded their heads.

"Don't you think a skunk is a pretty big surprise?" asked Lottie.

"It's the dumb cat's fault," said Hank.

"I want both of you to promise me that you will not cause any more trouble," said Aunt Lottie.

"I promise," said Charlie.

"Me too," added Hank. "We'll just practice roping."

Lottie's eyes brightened and she said, "Good, practice roping far away from the house and barn."

"I know," said Charlie grinning. "We'll go rope a unicorn for you."

"Perfect," said Aunt Lottie.

"We won't come back without a unicorn," promised Hank.

"I'm counting on it," said Aunt Lottie as the boys walked away.

"Let's go to my bedroom and get you into some cowboy clothes," said Hank.

While Charlie put on one of Hank's cowboy shirts, Hank pulled an old cowboy hat out of his closet and plopped it on Charlie's head.

"Now you look like a real buckaroo," said Hank. "Let's go to Butterfly Valley and rope some unicorns."

Hank saddled Tilly and grabbed his rope. He swung onto Tilly's back and Charlie climbed on behind him.

"How far is it to Butterfly Valley?" asked Charlie.

"It won't take long," said Hank. "I know a shortcut."

Hank's shortcut went through the neighbor's field, around an apple orchard, along a creek, up a hill, and into a grove of trees.

Hank pulled Tilly to a stop. He scratched his head and looked around.

"Are we lost?" asked Charlie.

"No," insisted Hank. "I just don't know where we're at or which direction to go."

A monarch butterfly landed on a tree right in front of Tilly. The little horse nudged the branch with her nose and the butterfly fluttered into the air.

"I'll bet she knows the way to Butterfly Valley," said Charlie, pointing at the brightly colored butterfly.

"You're a genius," said Hank, nudging Tilly into a trot.

Tilly followed the butterfly out of the trees, through a field of wildflowers, around a giant boulder, and to the top of a ridge.

On the crest of the hill, the boys looked down into Butterfly Valley. The meadow below seemed to be alive as hundreds of monarch butterflies fluttered their bright orange and black wings. Hank coaxed Tilly down the road into the valley.

Chapter 10

A Unicorn Named Pete

Butterflies fluttered around their heads as the boys rode through the tall milkweed flowers.

"Keep your eyes peeled for unicorns," said Hank. "They could be hiding anywhere."

Something moved in the flowers behind the boys.

"Did you hear that?" asked Charlie. "Something's following us. Maybe it's a unicorn."

Hank pulled Tilly to a stop and listened.

"I don't hear anything," said Hank.

He gave Tilly a nudge to continue into the milkweeds. Suddenly, there was a commotion behind them. A creature burst through the milkweeds and startled Tilly.

Tilly reared in the air before bucking and spinning in a circle. Hank and Charlie landed in a heap in the dirt and Tilly galloped away. Before Charlie could get to his feet he was being attacked by a long wet tongue.

"It's not a unicorn. It's a sheepdog," sputtered Hank.

Hank jumped up and hustled through the weeds to catch Tilly.

A curly-haired lady chased after the dog and said, "He won't hurt you. His name is Pete."

Charlie petted Pete's head and the shaggy dog rolled over on his back.

"I'm sorry," said the lady. "Pete gets a little overly excited sometimes. He loves to make new friends."

Hank came back leading Tilly through the milkweeds.

"Your dog nearly gave my horse a heart attack," said Hank.

"I'm truly sorry," said the lady. "My name is Lisa Monroe."

"I know," said Hank. "You're a teacher at my school."

Mrs. Monroe took a closer look at Hank and

smiled.

"Hank, I didn't even recognize you in your cowboy hat," said Mrs. Monroe.

"This is my cousin Charlie," said Hank.

"We're looking for unicorns," said Charlie. "We don't have time to chat."

"Do you have time for a cold soda? I have some root beers in the fridge," said Mrs. Monroe.

"Oh yeah," said Hank. "I'm pretty thirsty."

"Me too," added Charlie. "We've had a long ride."

The boys followed Mrs. Monroe through the milkweeds to a path that led to a house surrounded by a huge lawn.

Hank tied Tilly to a tree while Mrs. Monroe went into the cabin. She came back with three ice-cold root beers.

"Let's have a seat in the gazebo," said Mrs. Monroe.

She made her way over to an antique white, eight-sided structure that had a roof but no walls. Inside the gazebo were two benches.

"This is my favorite part of the property," said Mrs. Monroe. "I love to sit here and watch the butterflies."

"How come there are so many of them?" asked Hank.

"Because of the milkweeds," said Mrs. Monroe. "Monarch butterflies lay their eggs on milkweed plants. They migrate over three thousand miles every year."

"Their wings must get pretty tired," said Charlie.

"It takes four generations of butterflies to make the entire trip. They are magical creatures," said Mrs. Monroe.

"That's probably why they're best friends with unicorns," said Hank.

"Have you ever seen a unicorn?" asked Charlie.

"If you mean a mystical horselike creature with a long horn," said Mrs. Monroe. "No, I've never seen one of those. But to me unicorns are any rare creatures that embrace their differences and accept others for who they are. The magic isn't in the horn, it's in the heart. I believe a unicorn can be a dog, a cat, or even a person."

"My Aunt Lottie said my great-grandma was a unicorn," said Charlie. "She didn't have any hair and wore crazy eyebrows. But she loved everyone."

Mrs. Monroe pointed a finger to the sky and said, "She was a unicorn."

"That makes Ethel a unicorn," said Hank.

"Who's Ethel?" asked Mrs. Monroe.

"My pig," answered Hank. "She's nice to almost everyone, and it doesn't even bother her that she's a pig."

"Do you know what a group of unicorns is called?" asked Mrs. Monroe.

"A herd," guessed Hank.

"Nope," said Mrs. Monroe.

"A cornucopia?" guessed Charlie.

Mrs. Monroe laughed and said, "A group of unicorns is called a blessing. Isn't that perfect?"

"I like it," said Charlie. "I've got to tell Aunt Lottie. Unicorns are her lucky charms."

"What do you call a group of skunks?" asked Hank.

"That would be a surfeit," said Mrs. Monroe.

"Nope," said Hank. "They're called stinkers. We had a skunk spray in the barn where our Aunt Lottie is getting married tomorrow."

"It's her boyfriend's fault," added Charlie. "The skunk took one look at Rob's face and stunk up the whole place."

"Oh no!" said Mrs. Monroe. "Your aunt must be very disappointed."

"She's pretty upset," said Hank. "That's why we want to catch a unicorn and cheer her up."

Charlie looked at Butterfly Valley. He watched the butterflies fluttering as the sun began to set. He thought about how much he wanted Aunt Lottie to see it.

"Thank you for the root beer," said Charlie. "Can I ask one more favor?"

"Sure," said Mrs. Monroe.

"Would you let our Aunt have her wedding here? It would be so much better than a smelly barn," said Charlie.

Mrs. Monroe thought for a moment and then said, "I doubt your aunt would want to change locations at such short notice."

"If I can convince her, will you let her use your yard?" asked Charlie.

"You can tell your aunt that she's welcome to use my lawn and gazebo for her wedding. It would be my gift to the happy couple," said Mrs. Monroe.

While Hank untied Tilly, Mrs. Monroe went into her house. She came back with a slip of paper and handed it to Charlie.

"This is my cell number," said Mrs. Monroe. "Have your aunt give me a call if she decides to have her special day in Butterfly Valley."

The boys climbed on Tilly and soon they were galloping up the road to deliver the news. At the top of the hill Hank turned Tilly to take the shortcut home.

Chapter 11

The Best Blessing of All

When Hank and Charlie arrived back at the farm they were met by Hannah and Shrudi.

"You two are dead meat," said Shrudi. "You didn't tell anyone where you were going and it's almost dark."

"But we have great news," said Charlie.

"Nobody cares," said Hannah. "You're probably not even invited to the wedding anymore."

While Hank unsaddled Tilly, Charlie hurried into the house. When he came through the front door, he spotted his mom talking on her cell phone.

"They just got home," she said into her phone. "I will tell him."

She pushed the end button and turned to Charlie.

"Your father and Uncle Mike will be here soon. They have been looking all over for you," said Mom.

"We were at Butterfly Valley," said Charlie. "I need to talk to Aunt Lottie."

"Lottie and Rob are out looking for you too," said Mom. "You've had everyone worried."

A car pulled into the driveway. Charlie heard the car doors shut and soon Aunt Lottie burst into the room.

"I have great news," blurted Charlie.

Aunt Lottie didn't wait to hear the news. She hugged Charlie and said, "Thank you."

"You haven't heard the news yet," said Charlie.

Aunt Lottie interrupted Charlie and said, "I remembered you said you were going to rope a unicorn. That's when I put two and two together."

"Did you get four?" asked Charlie.

"No, I got Butterfly Valley," said Aunt Lottie. "We drove there to find you and I met Lisa Monroe. She told us you had asked her if we could have the wedding in her yard."

"What do you think?" asked Charlie.

"It's perfect," said Aunt Lottie. "It is the most magical place. The butterflies are amazing and the yard is gorgeous."

"And don't forget the unicorns," added Charlie.

With the exciting news about moving the wedding, Hank and Charlie's parents didn't punish the boys for being gone so long.

The next morning everyone was up early. They didn't have much time to get things ready at Butterfly Valley.

Aunt Sheila started texting the guests with the

change of location and directions to Butterfly Valley. Uncle Mike and Charlie's dad loaded the truck with the wedding flowers and decorations for the ceremony.

Lisa Monroe helped Mom and Aunt Lottie decorate the gazebo with flowers and twinkly lights. They laid out quilts in the yard for the guests to sit on.

Charlie got dressed in the tuxedo and asked Aunt Lottie, "How do I look?"

"Like a little prince," answered Lottie.

Charlie and Aunt Lottie watched as the guests started to arrive. Friends and family members laughed and greeted each other while they made their way to the quilts.

"Do you know what a group of unicorns is called?" asked Charlie.

Aunt Lottie smiled and said, "Yes, it's called a blessing."

"I think our family has a lot of unicorns in it," said Charlie.

"And that's the best blessing of all," said Aunt Lottie.

With butterflies fluttering around the gazebo, the wedding began. Rob and his best man walked across the grass first. They were followed by Hannah and Shrudi. The girls spread rose petals on the ground as they walked.

Charlie came next. He carried a small white pillow holding the two rings. He walked extra slow so that the rings wouldn't slide off the silk pillow.

He was halfway across the lawn when Pete came running out from behind the house. The shaggy dog raced up to Charlie. The crowd laughed as Charlie and Pete made their way to the gazebo.

When the music to "Here Comes the Bride" began playing, Aunt Lottie and Charlie's grandpa stepped out

of Lisa Monroe's house and onto her porch.

Charlie had never seen Grandpa dressed so fancy or looking so nervous. Aunt Lottie smiled the world's biggest smile as her father escorted her across the grass to the gazebo.

The ceremony was too long for Charlie's taste. He fidgeted back and forth while Rob and Lottie promised their love to each other.

After the vows, Charlie held the pillow up for Rob to take the rings. Rob and Lottie placed the rings on each other's fingers. Charlie covered his eyes when Rob gave Lottie a long kiss.

Suddenly, there was a commotion in the milkweeds. Charging through a cloud of monarch butterflies came Hank riding Tilly. He steered his prancing pony to the gazebo.

Hank did a quick dismount and waited while Rob

lifted Aunt Lottie into saddle. She rode side-saddle as Rob led Tilly through the cheering crowd.

Charlie turned to Hank and said, "When I grow up I'm going to marry a girl just like her."

"I thought you were never going to get married," said Hank.

Charlie smiled and said, "I changed my mind."

About the Author

Gary Hogg is the author of more than twenty books. His hilarious stories include *Look What the Cat Dragged In*, *I Heard of a Nerd Bird*, and the popular *Spencer's Adventures* series. Gary says his fourth grade teacher inspired him to put his wild ideas into stories instead of acting them out in class. She kept her sanity and he became a writer. Of all the characters he's created, Gary says Charlie Bacon is the most like him.

Gary is a popular speaker and guest author. He has inspired over 2 million students to be better writers with his popular *Writing is Exciting!* assembly and workshop program. You can learn about him at **www.garyhoggbooks.com**.